Cage Call

Life and death in the hard rock mining belt Photographs by Louie Palu with Essays and Interviews by Charlie Angus – the result of 12 years of documentary research conducted in the mining communities of Northeastern Ontario & Northwestern Quebec in Canada between 1991 and 2003

"Labour was the first price, the original purchase money that was paid for all things. It was not by gold or by silver, but by labour, that all wealth of the world was originally purchased...."

Adam Smith, The Wealth of Nations, 1776

Shaft miner at the 2500 foot level station before drilling, Louvicourt Mine, Val d'Or, Quebec.

Jumbo drills drilling a round in the shaft, 2500 foot level station, Louvicourt Mine, Val d'Or, Quebec.

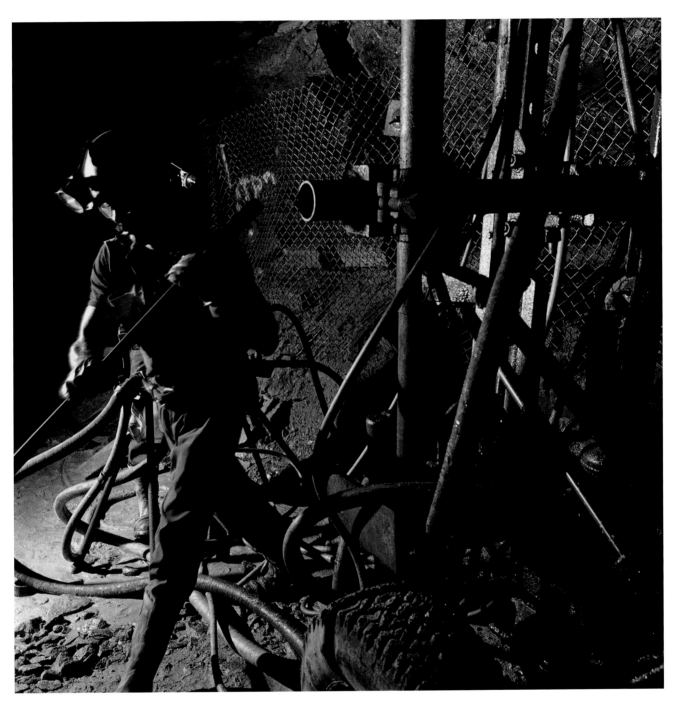

Changing steel on a longhole drill, 6750 foot level, Macassa Gold Mine, Kirkland Lake, Ontario.

Drilling a cross-cut on a ramp, 1750 foot level, Kerr Mine, Virginiatown, Ontario.

Drilling at the face in a sublevel, 1450 foot level, Kerr Mine, Virginiatown, Ontario.

Completion of drilling a breast in a shrinkage slope, 700 foot level, Cheminis Gold Mine, Larder Lake, Ontario.

Miners moving jackleg drills and gear before blasting in a shrinkage stope, 700 foot level, Cheminis Mine, Larder Lake, Ontario.

Miners entering the cage on surface for the beginning of day shift, Kerr Mine No. 3 Shaft, Virginiatown, Ontario.

A miner in the "Dry" hanging his work clothes in the air to dry after shift, Kerr Mine, Virginiatown, Ontario.

Exiting the cage on surface after graveyard shift, Kerr Mine No. 3 Shaft, Virginiatown, Ontario.

Snow covered houses and the McIntyre Mine No. 11 Shaft in Schumacher, Ontario.

Slag heaps, smoke stacks and blackened rock from decades of emissions from the Coniston Smelter, Coniston, Ontario.

Immigrant miners playing Bocce Ball in the Moneta neighbourhood, Timmins, Ontario.

Mine Mill Local 598 retiree at the union hall before a pensioners meeting, Sudbury, Ontario.

Boys snowboarding on a hill by Prospect Avenue, Cobalt, Ontario.

Tom Ranelli lifelong member of the Mine Mill Smelter Workers Union Local 598, the last Local of one of the most militant unions in North American history, Sudbury, Ontario.

A furnace tapper using a thermal lance to test the purity of molten nickel in the furnace, which operates at over 1000 degrees Celsius at the Falconbridge Smelter, Falconbridge, Ontario.

Converter aisle, Falconbridge Smelter, Falconbridge, Ontario.

Kerr Mine No. 3 Shaft headframe and crusher house, Virginiatown, Ontario.

Changing the hoist cable on the sheave wheel, atop the Kerr Mine No. 3 Shaft headframe, Virginiatown, Ontario.

Miner with "white hand", also known as Hand Vibration Syndrome, which is caused by working the drills.
It destroys circulation in the hands causing the hands to go numb, Kerr Mine, Virginiatown, Ontario.

Deckman in front of the Macassa Mine No. 3 Shaft, Kirkland Lake, Ontario.

Lunch break, 1450 foot level refuge station, Kerr Mine, Virginiatown, Ontario.

Scaling loose from the back, 1000 foot level, Cheminis Mine, Larder Lake, Ontario.

The late Lester Beattie smoking after drilling in a bypass drift, 1450 foot level Kerr Mine, Virginiatown, Ontario.

Rockbolting and screening below cable bolts prior to the 1993 rockburst, 6900 foot level, Macassa Mine, Kirkland Lake, Ontario.

Harold "Tubby" Burns holding a ladder at the exit of a shrinkage stope, 700 foot level, Cheminis Mine, Larder Lake, Ontario.

Ralph Schmidt and the late Guy Bruneau timbering a staging for drilling a breast in a shrinkage stope, 1300 foot level, Kerr Mine, Virginiatown, Ontario.

Tram crew Dave Effenberger and Claude "Shaggy" Ludgate having lunch on the 1300 foot level, Kerr Mine, Virginiatown, Ontario.

Larder Mens Wear, Larder Lake, Ontario.

Miners Pete Vaillant and David Butkevich members of the Mine Mill Union Hockey team at a union hockey tournament, Brampton, Ontario.

Shaft sinker Mario Gagnon (right) celebrating his last weekend in Canada at the Victory Tavern in Timmins, Ontario before leaving on a shaft sinking project in Mexico.

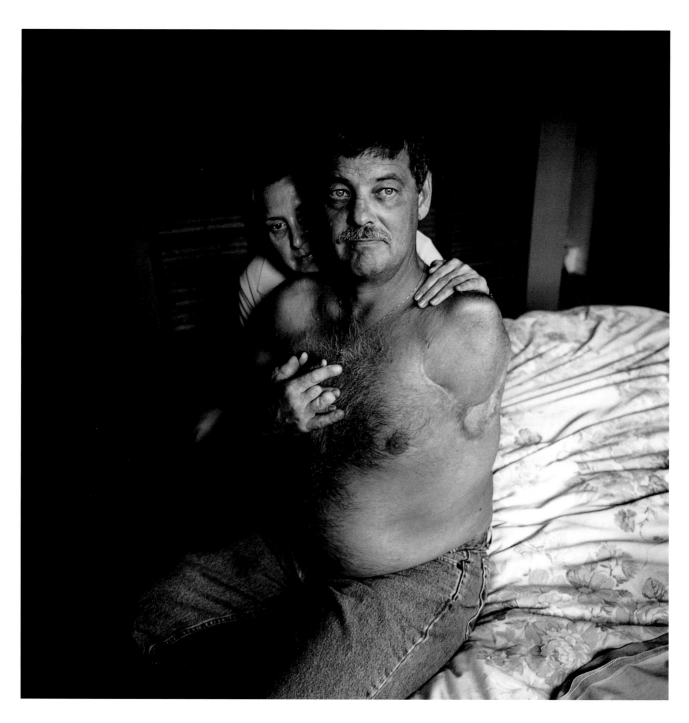

Landa Cormier with her husband Eric who lost his arm in an electrical accident at the Falconbridge Smelter, at their home in Garson, Ontario.

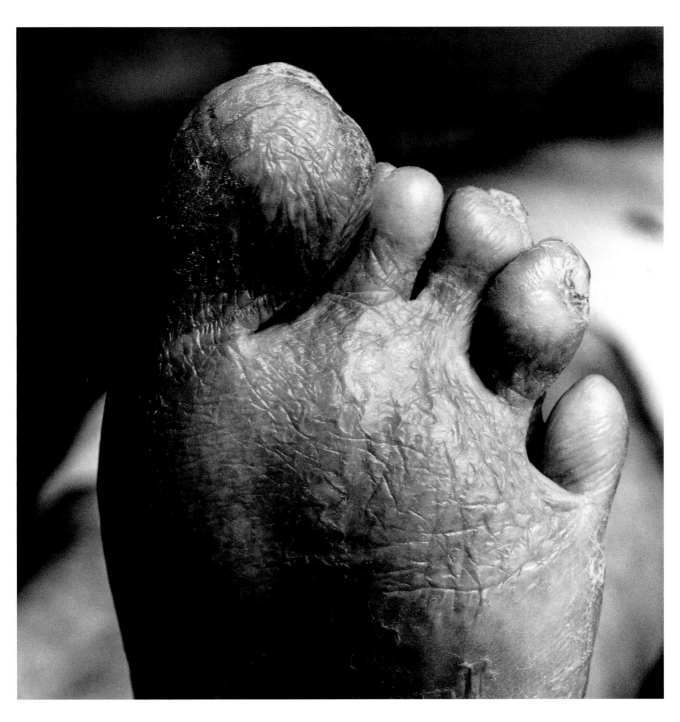

Former smelter mason Dwight Harper's foot which was severely burned by 1270 degree Celsius molten nickel in an accident at the Falconbridge smelter, seen at his home in Capreol, Ontario.

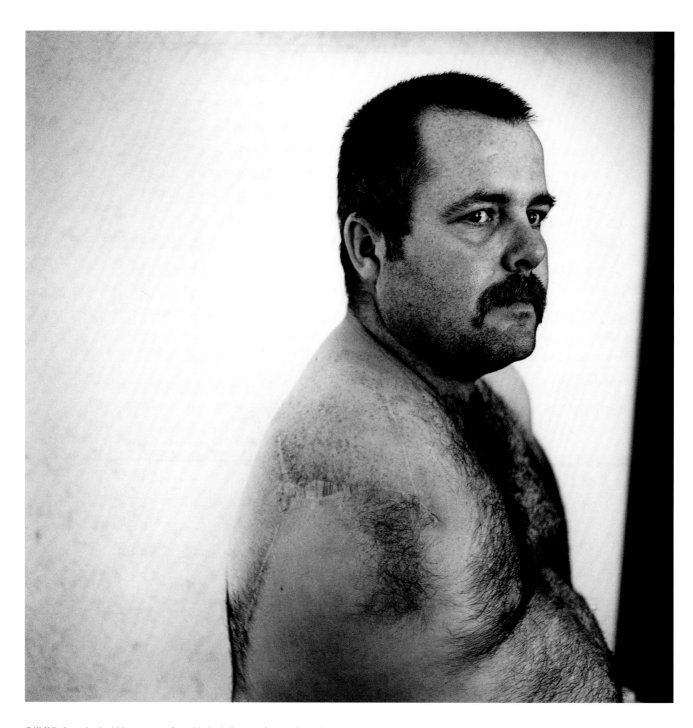

Bill Whelan who had his arm torn from his body by a surface rock crusher at the St. Andrews Mill, Timmins, Ontario.

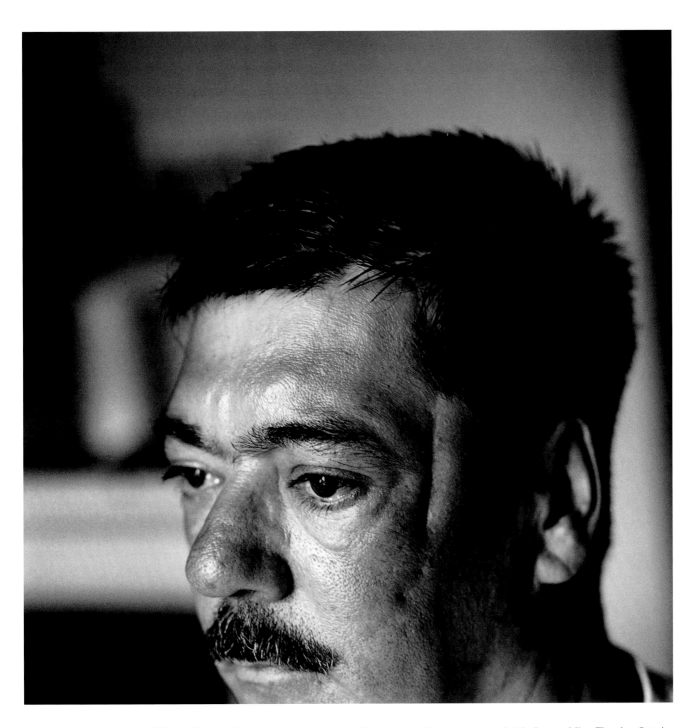

Bill Lee a former gold miner who was the victim of a severe head injury underground at the Pamour Mine, Timmins, Ontario.

An abandoned Russian Orthodox Church seen from a backyard in Kirkland Lake, Ontario.

The late John "Jack" Murnaghan, a retired union organizer holding a retirement gift which is a photo of the Macassa Mine where he worked for 43 years. At the time this photograph was taken, Murnaghan was living alone and suffering from Alzheimer's disease, Kirkland Lake, Ontario.

Retired mine labourer, 89 year old Willie Ciccone, playing the accordion at the Dante Club, Timmins, Ontario.

Gold miner's daughter Lise Bernatchez holding her son Julien. Her father Leonce Verrier was killed in the 1993 Macassa Mine rockburst.
It took 77 days to recover the body. Kirkland Lake, Ontario.

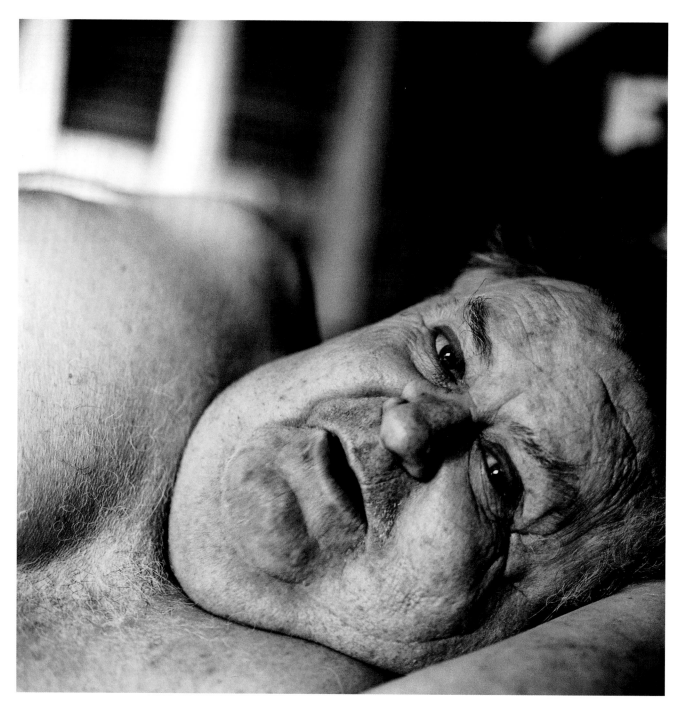

Hughie MacInnis, a paralyzed shaft miner lying in his bed. Hughie was paralyzed from the chest down following a shaft accident at Stobie Mine in 1975. Sudbury, Ontario.

Hughie MacInnis seen shaving in the mirror before attending church, Sudbury, Ontario.

21-year-old Carrie McKee with her one-year-old son Evan at the Miners Day of Remembrance. Her 20-year-old fiancé Chad Lamond was killed at the Creighton Mine in an underground accident when she was six months pregnant, Sudbury, Ontario.

Lola Angus on a grade school swing in the playground adjacent to the Right of Way Mine property, Cobalt, Ontario.

House on Union Street adjacent to the Inco Superstack, which is one of the tallest free standing smoke stacks in the world,
Copper Cliff Smelter Complex, Sudbury, Ontario.

House in Copper Cliff, Sudbury, Ontario.

Icicles on houses, Schumacher, Ontario.

Abandoned tailings pond and arsenic mine waste in a lake, Cobalt, Ontario.

Cage Call: Life and death in the hardrock mining belt
Text and Interviews by Charlie Angus

A Mining Town

I think the miners and their wives had a very true sense of community because they found out a lot quicker what life was all about. When they went into work they didn't know if they were coming home. And so they lived each day. Some people live a long time to learn this. If the sun rose today and it was a beautiful day to go ice fishing, they would go ice fishing. If someone was killed underground they didn't go into work that night. They sat in the bar and they talked about what a great guy he was and then they went out and looked after his wife and his children. They didn't wait for the government to look after them. They didn't wait for the company. They didn't wait for the union. They had a sense of living that I haven't seen in very many other people.

– Carrie Chenier, Elliot Lake, Ontario

Working at the Face

In the narrow confines of an underground gold stope, the sound of two drills tearing into the rock face is more than a sound; it is like a physical pounding against the body. The noise is amplified along the rock walls of the twisting cavern. The sound lets up slightly as one miner releases the pressure on the pneumatic support leg of the drill. He pulls the drill back far enough to release the drill steel from its retainer. A four-foot length of drill steel is pulled from the rock. Coolant water bleeds from the hole in the rock face. He grabs a longer steel rod, spears it into the hole, slaps down the retainer and bucks the drill back into the face.

The miners are drilling out a series of blasting holes on the face of the gold vein. At the end of their shift, the holes will be filled with AMEX blasting powder and wired to an electrical detonator. To maximize the speed with which they work, the miners store the various lengths of drill steel in the completed holes, giving the impression of a multitude of spears jutting from the rock. As the men sway back and forth in the misty oil spray of the drills, it's like watching Ahab taking down the whale.

The two men are partners, the primary production unit on which underground gold mining depends. A good partnership is based on skill, trust and an absolute intolerance for backsliders who don't have the drive to "give'er shit." Every move is done for maximum efficiency; two sets of arms, legs and eyes intent on making the cycle of a shift. The cycle is the ability to muck [shovel] out a blast; scale [scrape] the back [ceiling] for loose [rock]; apply metal screening and rock bolts along the back for safety; drill out a new round and get it set for blasting.

Jackleg mining is unforgiving work. It weeds out the mediocre in no time. The crews who succeed are driven by competive pride and the lure of the bonus [an incentive fee for ensuring production]. The best tend to be self-assured and cantankerous. As soon as the miners notice our lights behind them, they shut off the drills. Break time. Highballers [top bonus miners] don't like to work when a boss or visitor is watching them. This is their workplace. They'll handle the job without gawking witnesses.

When the machines are turned off, a remarkable stillness descends. And then the ear, which only moments ago was being battered at deafening volumes, suddenly becomes attuned to the minimalist soundscapes of the dark; the lonely plunk of work boots in mud, the eerie ping of water dripping through spider-like fissures in the rock and the unmistakable groan of millions of tonnes of earth shifting above.

At 3,700 feet underground the sound of the earth shifting its weight following a blast or the removal of ground support is remarkably similar to the snap of a dry branch. This tension crack in the rock is an unnerving sound – enough to make you glance furtively over your shoulder. The rational mind knows that there is nothing to fear. After all, the development of an underground mine is based on scientific engineering principles. State-of-the-art computer modeling anticipates the response of ground stress on the particular geologic fault lines and rock formations of the mine.

But even the most complex computer-modeling scenario will only take a man so far as he stands alone in the darkness of the earth. To an old school miner, it doesn't matter how many university degrees some "suit" has as they point to a computer screen to explain the reliability of a section of ground. The miner will always rely on what his instincts tell him. He knows how to read the rock. He knows when his skin starts to tingle. And he listens closely to the way a particular mine speaks. Every mine has its own personality. The cracking, knocking and spitting of the rock helps

reveal what the earth is thinking. As a veteran miner will tell you, never trust ground that is silent because you can't guess what it will do.

As a mine advances deeper into the earth, the sounds change. Ground pressure dramatically increases as one passes the one-mile mark underground. At 7,000 feet in the Creighton Deep Nickel Mine, for example, the sound of the earth releasing tension is much more invasive than the snap of a branch. It's like standing beside two boxcars as they bump hard against each other in a rail yard.

Little wonder that miners call such occurrences the "bumps." Since the earliest days, miners have sung songs about the bumps, told tales about them and even personified them as the goblin forces of the deeps. What is particularly unnerving about this phenomenon is that you can never locate the source of the bumping. But it's there like an angry neighbour pounding on the rock walls, letting you know that you have no business being there.

In the Creighton Deep Mine, the bumps are so invasive they can be heard above the hurricane shriek of cold air as it whistles through the ventilation tubes into the oppressive heat of the working face. And yet, despite the racket, the Creighton miners casually go about their work. They know that even if the ground is cranky it is not necessarily malevolent.

Such calm assuredness in a cavern a mile and a half below surface is a relatively new phenomenon. For much of the 20th century, the ability to breach the notorious 7,000-foot barrier was little more than a mine owner's fantasy. Oh sure, there were some mines who attempted to chase the veins into the depths but intense ground pressure and suffocating heat snuffed out these fledgling experiments. In the 1960s, the Lake Shore Gold Mine tried mining high-grade gold at depth but as one veteran put it: "At 8,000 feet I shook hands with the devil."

The 120-year-old Creighton Mine has broken the depth barrier thanks to the continual innovation in new technologies. Jumbo drills, operated from air-conditioned cabs, have replaced the handheld jackleg drills. Robotic longhole drills and remote control scoop trams [diesel shovel loaders] can be operated from the safety of surface buildings. A complex ventilation plant, with a cost estimated to be around $60 million, has been installed to pump ice-cold air into depths that would otherwise be an oppressive 112 degrees Fahrenheit.

Creighton Deep is typical of the technological innovation that is renewing the historic mining regions of the Canadian Shield. All across the vast, armadillo-like rock terrain of northern Canada there are numerous communities that were built on the discovery of deposits of gold, silver, nickel, copper, iron or uranium. In these isolated ouposts life was hard but the families forged a strong cultural sense of identity with their sports teams, dance bands and community halls based on ethnic, social or union affiliations.

The wealth from these deposits gave birth to many of the mining corporations that came to dominate international mining exploration in the 20th century. As these companies moved investment overseas, many of the home communities atrophied; some from depleted ore bodies, others because their mines couldn't compete against low cost competition coming on stream in the Third World. As the residents of any mining community will tell you, a company's flag of origin is no basis for loyalty in a world judged strictly by tonnages.

High wages and strict environmental laws have placed many aging Canadian mining regions at a distinct disadvantage compared to competing operations in South America, Africa or the former republics of the Soviet Union. Canadian miners must compete, ounce for ounce and tonne for tonne, against Third World operations where mountains can be stripped bare by giant hydraulic shovels.

Mining has always been a global game and innovation is the key to survival. The ever-elusive ore bodies are being mapped out with cutting-edge computer mapping technologies. Today's miners are no longer low-paid grunts, but highly paid specialists with wages unmatched by other blue-collar work. Robotics, automation and advancements in ground mechanics have made the safety standards in Canadian mines the envy of the world.

But innovation only goes so far. At the end of the day, mining is based on the luck of a geological draw that was determined millions of years ago. The mining gods are arbitrary in whom they bless and whom they curse. This is the way it has always been for prospectors, communities and the miners at the face. No other industry so clearly illustrates the direct relationship between the physical costs paid by labour to the benefit of international monetary empires. In its starkest sense, mining remains a world of winners and losers. Those who lose tend to lose big time, which is why mining has never been just a job. It is a distinct culture with a shared sense of history, traditions and superstitions.

Miners romanticize the long shot chance in the lottery of fate but they know that they, like the ground they mine, remain bound by the laws of entropy. The good times never last. Every tonne mined brings even a great mine one tonne closer to its death. And sooner or later, the mines will claim the strength of the strongest miner. June Nash captured this Faustian reality of mineral exploitation in the title of her study of Bolivian tin miners: "We Eat the Mines and the Mines Eat Us" [Columbia University Press, 1982].

For the miners of northern Canada, the implications of such a bargain ingrains a dualistic worldview – a relentless optimism that another deposit will be found, combined with a "devil may care" determination to live for today. Their lore is full of colourful tales of the highballers who defy the odds by living and playing as hard as they work. After all, what other job is there where a man spends his whole shift making his work place safe only to blow it up at the end of the day?

But there is another element to be considered pondering the cultural tendency of miners and mining communities to live for the day. At the end of the shift, the very act of riding to surface in the cage is, in itself, an act of resurrection. Having spent the day in the diesel-tainted air of underground, a miner's first taste of fresh air on surface is a moment to be savoured. He spends his days in darkness, only to return to a world of the night sky.

Which is why when the miners turn off their drills and ride the cage back to surface, you're liable to find them spending their time in the outdoors. On Saturdays they'll be out on their boats bombing around the cold, deep waters of northern lakes. Basking in sunshine. Living in the moment.

Brothers. Comrades. Buddies.
Blaring AC/DC tunes.
Catching fish.
Not worried about the next cage call into the depths.

Going Underground

I started at Kerr Gold Mine in my last year of high school in 1982. I told myself I'd work a summer and save up enough money to buy a car and then quit. But it never happens. You get used to the money. All five boys in my family went underground.

– Steve Sheldon, Larder Lake, Ontario

School of Life

I quit school in Grade 5 and went to work with my dad and Charlie Dean hauling leftover pieces of cobalt ore out of the remains of the old Nipissing [processing] Mill in Cobalt [Ontario]. We hauled it out in wheelbarrows and I made four dollars a day. When I turned 14, I went to work in the kitchen of the Temagami Copperfields Mine. At 17 I went underground at the Cobalt Lode Mine. It was February 10, 1957. The Mine Captain said I looked young for my age. I told him that I had 12 brothers and sisters at home to feed. There were many times when we were hungry at the kitchen table.

The first job I had underground was digging ditch. You had to fill a one-tonne ore car with a shovel. They expected me to do five cars a day but I soon got it up to eight cars a day. From hand mucking I went to pulling ore chutes. The only training you got was to watch a guy for about four days and then you were expected to be able to do it. I then learned to be a machine[drill] man, a drift man, a raise man.

I've worked for all the big contractors - Redpath, Cloutier from Rouyn, Ram Raising and Paddy Harrison. The reason they have contractors is that there's a lot of work in a mine that regular miners won't do. A contractor will do the work about three times faster than a company man can do it. The contractor will hire a guy off the streeet. If, after six months, he doesn't get hurt, that's great. They'll put him into the good ground where he makes good bonus. But there's no pension. No security. No nothing.

Do the contractors skirt safety rules? Absolutely. 100%. You never see a company safety officer checking a [blasting] round that's been done by a contractor. The companies know these guys aren't following the rules. If the job has to be done, even if it's not safe, the contractor will do it. Don't refuse to do the job because you'll be sent down the road.

– Jerry Stewart, Haileybury, Ontario

Drift Miner in a Gold Mine

The Star Club was a boarding house near the Dome Mine. The first men to be fed were the shaft sinkers, then the drift and the raise men, then the stope men and then the timber men. The last man to get fed was the shit man [underground outhouse cleaner]. The hierarchy of the mine extended into the community. What was said on the mine during one shift was talked about all through town by the next morning. The gossip line was called the Dome telephone.

Now there just isn't the sense of community that we used to have in the mines. You can see it from all the beer parlours closing down. The beer parlour was our social centre. It was the place we went to meet and socialize. We didn't have video games or computers. The idiot box changed our entire social structure. As well, there's a completely different kind of person underground today. I could make a miner in half an hour today. There's no skill needed.

People see miners as little more than animals. But the old style of mining took 90% brains and 10% brawn. In a jackleg stope you had to be able to plan six months ahead. It's the same with drift [tunnel development] mining. Everything is done in careful steps over a long period while the rest of the mine is carrying the costs of this development.

You have to know how to read the rock. There's a grain to the rock just as there is a grain to wood. You have to hit it a certain way if you want to break it. The rock never welcomes you but it accepts you. Dome Mine was good because the ground was hard sedimentary rock. The veins twist 75 or 80 degrees and it's easy to read the rock. You can watch the cuttings coming out of the drill to know if you're on the vein or not.

But those quartz veins are hard on the lungs. Quartz is like flying glass. We had a guy who lost a foot because a piece of quartz was in his boot and it worked his way into his foot and at the end of the shift they couldn't get it out.

I worked on shaft jobs and in the drifts. I preferred to work in the drifts because if you didn't like a situation you get out. At the bottom of a shaft, if something goes wrong you have no place to go – all you can do is pray you don't get hit.

A miner doesn't get scared. If he does he won't be a miner for long. I remember the day the heart went out of me. It was in a raise when loose started raining down on us. There was about three seconds of hearing these pieces of loose falling down towards us and knowing there was no place to hide. It terrified me enough to change my life. After that I went from being a good miner to an all right miner.

– Hugh Vallance, South Porcupine, Ontario

Raise Miner

In the 1950s, I went to work as a raise miner. A raise is generally sloped at 45 degrees and connects the levels of the mine. The opening to the raise was very tiny so you always had to work alone. Raise mining was the most dangerous because, after a blast, you never knew what was hanging up there. You could be injured by falling rock while climbing back up to your workplace. Then once you were up there, you had to wedge yourself against the wall and use a steel bar to try and knock down all the loose rock. Then you'd build a little wooden platform to mount your drill on while you got ready to take another round out. All this was very jerry-rigged and quickly thrown together and sometimes the vibrations could shake the platform loose. Raise mining paid about eight or 10 cents an hour more than any other mining and so we liked to work in the raise.

– Reg Doan, North Bay, Ontario

Veterans of the Long War

There's a little white house sitting beside the twisting line of asphalt that runs along Highway 112 into the gold mining town of Kirkland Lake, Ontario. On this stretch of the road, pretty much all the houses look alike - white vinyl boxes, barely noticed in a landscape of snow and evergreens.

Over mugs of instant coffee at the kitchen table, Glenda and Pete Saille are telling me about the African parrots. The birds are perched in the kitchen watching me with disinterested disdain. I'm just another biped mugging and quacking in front of them in the vain hope of eliciting a response. It doesn't work.

The dog knows better. He won't go anywhere near the birds. And the cat... "Well," says Pete, "every time the cat comes in the house, the birds start to chant, 'Let's kill the cat. Let's kill the cat.'"

If Glenda's cooking spaghetti one of the birds will fly over to the stove.

"Polly's hungry," the bird says.

"Too hot for Polly,'" Glenda replies.

The bird responds, "Polly wants some now."

"Polly will have to wait."

"Oh ya?" says the bird. "Well, fuck you bitch."

Glenda breaks into laughter every time she tells the story.

It's too much to believe. But Glenda's not a bullshitter. Neither is her husband Pete. And they don't really care whether you believe the stories. What's true is what happened.

The birds belong to their boarder, Wilson "Newfie" Lambert. He spends his week working 140 km up the road at the Kidd Base Metal Mine. He comes home on the weekend for a comfort meal from Glenda and to trade tales with his old buddy Pete. Newfie has been mining for years, but other than the parrots and a pickup truck, he doesn't have much to show for the years.

This is the way Pete explains it: "When the timber crew at the mine shouts down the hole, 'Timber going down,' Newfie shouts back, 'Alimony going up.'"

"He lost the house and everything to his wife," Glenda says. "But he don't care. He says he can't fit a house into a packsack."

The term "packsack miner" dates back to the days of the 19th century mining rushes of the western United States. Packsack miners were independent blasters and drillers who travelled from mining region to mining region, selling their skills, never putting down roots. Today's packsack miners work as hired guns for elite contract companies. The contractors bid on the difficult jobs of building new mines or advancing the underground infrastructure in existing operations.

Pete Saille spent a number of years working as a contractor. The name of the game was making the most out of the bonus system.

"In a sub drift [access tunnel for a cut and fill stope] you might get paid 75 bucks a foot for advance. Say you break seven feet in a blast, you deduct wages off for two men and whatever left is bonus. A lot of places you have to pay for all your own tools. Now if you lose a diamond drill bit in a hole and can't get it out – well that's $600. You can forget about your bonus because you'll be paying it off for the rest of the month. But we'd go in and sweat to make the cycle in five hours. We were making $34 an hour in bonus when the wage was $17 an hour."

Much bigger money was available to the tough few who could get hired on inter-national shaft sinking and development crews. Canadian contractors are at the top of the pecking order in the international world of mine development. Pete signed on for a job that took him around the world.

"We lived like goddamned kings overseas," he says. "We were making $7,500 a month [1970s and 1980s]. We'd come home and buy a new car and have only two months to drive it before being shipped out again."

Top money was paid to the shaft sinking crews. Pete took down Creighton No. 9 with the legendary Irish-Canadian contractor Paddy Harrison. When it came time for the sinking of Macassa No. 3 in Kirkland Lake, Pete was the natural choice as shaft leader. At the time [1983-86] the sinking of the 7225-foot shaft was the deepest mine project in the western hemisphere. Any veteran from that job is quick to throw out the stats of footage blasted, tonnes hauled and cement poured. Glenda, however, is ready with her own set of stats.

"There were 283 men hired during the sinking of that shaft. By the time the job was done over 180 had separated from their wives."

Why?

She just laughs slyly. "You know how they are...they're hardrock miners."

She doesn't feel the need to connect the dots of the shaft miner's notoriety for wild living. Instead, Glenda produces another of set of statistics; she claims there were only seven guys who managed to stay on the job from the beginning of the contract until it was completed.

"They told the men to expect two fatalities on a shaft of this scale," she says.

Dave Whiddifield was the first fatality. He was squeezed to death when he got caught on the cross head of the No. 2 ore bucket and was dragged up into the shaft timbers.

Pete nearly became the second fatality. He was hit in a rock burst [exploding rock from ground pressure] when the crew was blasting out the benches [a blast section in a shaft] below 5500 level. He was buried alive when the rockburst brought the shaft walls down on him.

The rockburst happened on the very first day his teenage son joined the crew to go underground.

"My son had only been underground for two hours when the blast hit me. He never wanted to go back underground after that. But I made him go back. He didn't want to."

Why would a parent send their son back underground into the dangerous world of shaft sinking?

"You gotta go back," Glenda says. "What else are you going to do? It's like falling off a horse."

After a year undergoing medical rehabilitation, Pete returned to work as a shaft contractor. "I went back with a gold plaque from the company and a lot of steel bolted in my damned leg."

In the late 1990s, a 2,500-foot shaft was begun on the Victoria Creek gold deposit in Northeastern Ontario. Pete was the leader on the project. Part of his duties included regular inspections of the shaft and surface headframe [the elevator building above the shaft]. During one inspection he stepped out on the timbers after giving the hoistman a signal to halt all traffic in the shaft. For some reason that signal wasn't received, and as Pete began his inspections, he was smashed by a passing ore bucket. The crew found him hanging onto the mine timber 80 feet off the ground. His pelvis was crushed.

The doctors told Pete he'd never walk again. He spent months lying in bed looking at his seemingly dead legs. And then one day it happened, he saw his toe move.

Over the next year, Pete slowly but methodically learned to walk again. But he never went back to work. Most of his time now is spent puttering around the house doing little projects.

"I have good days and I have bad days," he says, shrugging off the constant pain in his hips.

Pete stills loves to talk mining. He wants to know what I've seen of the Kidd D [deep] shaft sinking project. "They're taking the shaft below 10,000 feet," he says wistfully.

It's clear he still longs to be back in the heart of the action.

"Sure I miss it when I get together with the boys." He then pauses and pats his damaged pelvis. "But all those young bucks....I couldn't compete against them anymore."

"Ah hon," says Glenda affectionately. "You could dance circles around them."

She then nudges Pete to take me out to the garage and show me his favourite toy – a black sports car. The car is kept carefully protected from the long, hard winters. Come summer, Pete will take it for a spin along the two-lane highway into town. A sports car and African parrots – leftover booty of a packsack miner.

Smelter Town

Coniston was an Inco [International Nickel Company] town. We lived in a company house. My grandfather would walk to work at the smelter from where he lived in Coniston. All my uncles worked for Inco as did my grandfather. He had come over from the old country [Italy] and was active in the union. He used to pull me out of school and we'd go fishing and he would talk about the importance of the union and the CCF [Co-operative Commonwealth Federation – a farm/labour party].

It was always a big thrill to go down to the smelter and watch them dump the [molten] slag. The slag dumps were where teenagers went for a romantic evening to watch the fireworks on the hill. It was like hanging out at the drive-in.

My uncle used to ride the back of the slag train as a switchman. One night my dad set it up so that my uncle would take me and my brother for a ride on the slag train. I was about 12 at the time. We went out in January and it must have been -30. It was freezing. We rode on the back of the train with my uncle. When we reached the dump site he got out with the sledgehammer. They had to dump quickly before the slag cooled and caked to the sides of the car. He pounded on the cars and the slag that was starting to cool would fall out like big chunks. He would pound the 10 or 15 cars on the train and then head back to the smelter for another load. He did this all night.

As I watched him, he said, "This is what a man does for a living."

I turned 18 in 1972 and went down to sign up at Inco. They gave you a choice whether to start at the smelter or underground. I remember hearing my grandfather and uncles coughing all the time from working in the smelter so I said I wanted to work underground. I started out as a ditch digger in the old Frood Mine. My grandfather then took me down to the union hall and I signed my first union card; three months later I was a steward.

– Wayne Glibbery, Coniston, Ontario

From the Old Country

I came from Ukraine as a young girl. My husband went to work at Frood Mine in 1942. The Ukrainians were known as hard workers but nobody who was ethnic had any job of responsibility at Inco. No matter how good you were or how long you worked there, you were always by passed for promotion. My husband was very physical. He worked hard.

Sudbury wasn't a very pleasant place to look at back then. We used to go out and pick mushrooms, blueberries and wild cranberries. But there would be dust storms coming off the tailings [mine waste]. And when the sulphur fumes came down from the smoke stack we'd have to run out and run water on the garden to keep the sulphur from burning the vegetables.

There was a lot of conflict in Sudbury then. There was no mixing between Ukrainian Catholics and Ukrainian Orthodox in Sudbury. There was also a big divide between Ukrainians who came here before the war and Ukrainians who came after the war. Some of the new people were very ready to fight for nationalism in Ukraine but the older groups wanted to have nothing to do with anything that hinted of the life before. The other big division in the Ukrainian community was between those who supported the Mine Mill [and Smelter Workers] Union and Ukrainians who supported the Steelworkers Union. Mine Mill was seen as more socialist. The dividing line between communities was very prominent. It was the same in the Serbian and the Croatian communities.

Life was better than it had been on the farm. We weren't isolated. We had people from the same background and so we had support. If you worked hard you got a pay cheque. We thought, "Hey, this is good."

My husband and I never went back to Ukraine. Why go back? There's nothing there for us.

– Mary Martyn, interview conducted in Ukranian through the translation of her son at St. Vladimir's Orthodox Church, Sudbury, Ontario

Life in the Moneta

It is late summer and the patchwork backyards of the Moneta have produced a rich bounty of fresh tomatoes, cucumbers and beans. Soon the local men will get together for the annual making of sausage and homemade wine. It's always been this way in the Moneta (Italian slang for money), the Italian neighbourhood on the south side of Timmins, Ontario. The Moneta is dotted with small butcher shops and local watering holes with the two pillars of the community being the Italian Dante Social Club and the Sacred Heart Church with its Sunday morning-mass in Italian.

The Italian community in Timmins dates back to the first gold rush of 1909 when Leo Mascioli, a construction contractor, began bringing workers over from his home region of Abruzzia. The migration continued until the early 1960s. But the Italian character of the neighbourhood remains strong because the children and grandchildren of the Italian miners have planted deep roots in the Moneta.

Angela and Alfredo Ciccone are typical of the people who came to this land of harsh winters and short summers. "We came over here in 1959 from Abruzzia," says Alfredo. "I came from a farm. I had never seen a mine before."

Without a trade or the ability to speak English, Alfredo went to work underground as a labourer at the McIntyre Gold Mine.

"I started on the track gang [laying railway track for underground cars] at the McIntyre. I couldn't speak English. Nobody told me what to do. I cried lots in those early days. I wanted to quit but a German guy told me not to worry. He said I'd make it and he began to show me what to do."

In 1963, top money at the mine was the $35 a day being made by the miners working in drift development. These crews would bid against each other for contracts based on how much ground they could cover. The company paid them a bonus based on how much footage could be drilled. Alfredo watched the drift miners carry out their trade. In time he worked up his nerve to bid on a drift mining contract.

"When I started in the drift we had to blast 11-foot [deep] rounds in 10' x 10' tunnels. Nobody told you how to do it right. If you didn't make your blast you didn't come up at the end of your shift. You kept working until it was done. You didn't have time to eat lunch. You ate your lunch on the way down or when you were coming back up."

A new drill crew was given just a few chances to learn how to make the break – the particular sequence of hole spacings and timed blasts to force an opening in the hard, granite textures of the pre-Cambrian shield rock.

The central break consisted of six carefully chosen holes drilled in the centre of the rock face. Then followed a series of symmetrical drill patterns spreading out from the central break. Success depended on timing the sequence of the explosive "shots." If, for example, the four holes at the top of the face were the last to detonate, the pressure forced the broken rock into the ground, making it harder to muck out. The best blast was timed so that the bottom charges went off slightly after the central and upper charges, pushing the rock upwards for the convenience of the mucking shovels.

It was precision work. The miner had to cut and tie each fuse length – shorter for the blasts that opened the cut, longer for the charges to follow in sequential pattern. He then had to light each fuse and then scramble for safety, hoping that all charges would go off. The worst fear was having to go back into a drift to examine a blast that failed to go off or deal with bootlegs [failed charges] that were still in the face at the beginning of the next round of drilling. Misfirings and miscalculations resulted in numerous mining injuries and deaths over the years. At the very least, mistakes in blasting resulted in headache causing delays. Any mistakes were charged against the miner's account.

"If you didn't make the break, you didn't make any money," Alfredo says matter of factly. "The company didn't give you nothing. You paid for everything you needed."

The men covered the cost of their own blasting powder and blasting caps. They sharpened their own drill steels. They paid for their work oilers - none of which

lasted more than a month.

"We were working in areas where there was so much water pouring on us that we had to cut holes in our oilers to keep them from filling up."

Now retired from the mines, he is still passionate about the skills he acquired underground, but he's more passionate about talking about his garden. He is proud of this little patch of land just as he is proud of his daughters – Angela and Roberta. They are teachers. They have soft hands and educated minds. They consider themselves Canadian. And as much as Alfredo dreams of going home to the warm lands of Abruzzia he is content to stay here in the Moneta, a place that he now calls home.

"We had nothing when we came here," he says. "Today this country will only take people with college degrees and computer knowledge. Even the mines are like that. We would starve if we came here today. All's we had was our willingness to work. And we made a good life."

Three Unions - Two Generations

My dad beat a firing squad in Finland. In the 1918 Civil War, a friend of his who was on the other side saw his name on the hit list and warned him. My dad escaped to Denmark and then over to North America. He started in the mines in the Coeur d'Alenes [Idaho] and then worked his way up into Montana.

He was involved in union activities in the mining camps in the United States back in the days of the Western Federation of Miners. He told me stories about this big Swedish guy who was very prominent in the mining union in Montana. His wife ran a laundry doing the miners' clothes.

The Ku Klux Klan were working with the Pinkertons [Detective Agency] for the company. They burnt a cross on his front lawn and told him to get the hell out of town. He went down to the hardware store and bought three or four 30-30 rifles and ammunition. Sure enough, the cops disappeared and the KKK showed up and shot his house and the laundry all to rat-shit. His wife was loading the 30-30s while he was firing back. The battle went on for about four hours and not a cop came around. But both he and his wife survived.

It was civil war, plain and simple. One mine manager, who was a real prick, hired the Pinkertons to take the union out. The Pinkertons were little more than hit men. So the miners decided to kill him. The WFM had their own "powder men" for jobs like this. This manager used to walk across the vacant lot to the headframe every day and they set this dynamite charge to kill him. They caught the wrong guy. My father had real sorrow about what happened.

My father left the States to work in the gold fields of Kirkland Lake and then went to Inco at Sudbury. He got black-listed at Creighton Mine in 1932 for union activity. Then he got a job at [Inco's] Levack Mine under an assumed name. Somebody squealed on him and that was it. From that point on, he couldn't get a job in mining at all.

I went to work for Inco when I was 18. I started in the Copper Cliff smelter working on the converter aisle. There were six cranes going continuously carrying [molten] matte and slag ladles above our heads. It was the closest thing to hell you'd get on Earth. We had no helmets. I wore a fedora. I started in May and saw two guys burnt to death in early June. The big hook on the crane broke and this ladle of hot slag fell, hit the transfer car and tipped. The guys started to run but the slag just washed them down. All that was left were two beautiful grease stains on the concrete floor. I stood there in absolute horror, absolute horror. The slag was so hot that their boots had turned to charcoal and they had to run hoses over the stain for a long time before they could go in and get what was left of the bodies.

After three months I joined the union and became a steward. Mine Mill [the direct descendant of the Western Federation of Miners] was the union at Inco then. But Mine Mill just didn't have any money in the bank to fight Inco. We had come through the '58 strike and the union was broke and the miners were bitter and demoralized. I realized that the only goddamned way we could fight Inco was to have the whole labour movement in North America behind us. For that, we needed the strength of the Steelworkers [United Steelworkers of America]. My father and I had a really bitter argument about me supporting Steel in the raids against Mine Mill. My whole family was loyal to Mine Mill.

I became one of the key Steel organizers at Creighton Mine which was full of Mine Mill supporters. Steel sytematically took control of the Mine Mill turf, one bar at a time. My brother owned the Waters Hotel which was where all the Creighton miners and a lot of the smelter workers drank. I would walk into that bar and my brother would tell me to fuck off. My brother-in-law was the bouncer; when I'd start getting into it with the Mine Mill supporters he'd say, "Drink your beer and get the fuck out of here, or I'll throw you out."

In the end, the battle was decided by a vote of Inco workers in 1962 when 14,333 workers voted and the Steelworkers won by just 15 votes. They counted all night. I think there were five recounts.

The Mine Mill battle against Steel has to be one of the most heroic battles in labour history. They had such limited resources and were so badly outgunned in the face of Steel's unlimited funds. To lose that vote by 15 votes shows how much guts and determination they had.

– Jack Rauhala, Sudbury, Ontario

The Great Awakening

Miners are a funny breed. Even the educated miners. You get a guy who comes out of school and gets put in a drift where he's making two or three hundred bucks a day. He's never seen that kind of money. He's on top of the world. He buys all his toys, eats in restaurants every night. When the time comes where he can't keep up any more he'll have nothing. No truck. Just an old car. I don't know if people are like that in other jobs, but miners know that even if the work is bad for them, they'll still do it.

A miner will try and beat his own record every day and work like a fucking dog – knowing the work is doing him in, knowing he's getting slower. Part of the fast aging process in miners comes from the lack of sunlight. In winter he'll go on shift and not be exposed to sunlight for nine or ten days straight.

He'll eat his lunch running a drill machine with oil mist spraying on the sandwich. That's how these guys get stomach cancer. I'd tell these guys, "Don't waste your life for the overtime or the bonus." But you know what the guys say, "[You can] go home, sleep with my wife, drink my last beer but don't touch my bonus."

I was an underground diesel mechanic with 23 years experience and I was making 19 bucks an hour at Pamour Mine. It wasn't great pay but we had good bargaining language. We fought for pensions and braces for the kids.

People died bringing the unions into the mines. Then, over time, the unions got in with management. The company would give the union president steady day shifts and paid for his office. They paid for the time it took to handle negotiations.

But then the mining companies expanded into places like Indonesia and South Africa. As soon as they saw what men over there were willing to put up with, they had the great awakening. Suddenly they thought, why should we be buying these guys boots and clothing when miners overseas will put up with fuck all? Now it's like "fuck you, pay for your own fucking negotiations."

Pamour had always been a profitable little mine until Peggy Witte [president of Royal Oak Mines] came along and bought the mine in the early 1990s. Peggy brought in her own team of managers and everything started to go downhill. There was no loyalty. They didn't care who you were. They didn't know my dad. They never went to school with your mom. You meant nothing to them. A guy has 10 years in at the mine and there's a problem? Get rid of him. The first thing they tried to do when they came to Pamour was to break the family but they never succeeded.

Royal Oak stripped everything out of the mine to pay for their investments in the Kemess Mine in British Columbia, which was a total white elephant. It got so bad we were having to go into old headings to steal parts to keep our machines going. Everything was second hand. We'd rebuild the motors as good as new but when you're running a diesel scoop in a heading with no clean air it's going to burn black. It's contaminated air being run through the machine and coming out as more contaminated air. It didn't matter if you rebuilt an engine 15 times.

Try and get a new ventilation fan for a guy and they'd cry like it was going to make them go broke. There'd be no friggin' air in some headings. The scoops would be eating it all and the jacklegs would be taking it. We brought in a health specialist into one heading where this guy was working and she said the air was the equivalent of smoking 5,000 packs of cigarettes a day. And the company didn't want to put in a fan into this heading because it cost too much.

When the company finally collapsed in 1999, the lawyers moved in and seized the assets. We then found that the company had been raiding the pension fund. When the mine was closed, I had only 13 years left to go for a pension and now have nothing to show for it. I'll have to work until I'm 70 at this rate.

It used to be that it wasn't a big thing to see the union president sitting down with the company president in the beer parlour having a beer on a Saturday afternoon at the hotel. Now that would never happen. Never,never,never, never!

The thing about Pamour was that whether it was the guys working in the drifts, the raises or the mechanics shop, we were all brothers. We had baseball and hockey tournaments, family get-togethers. Everybody was everybody's keeper. But you know, after all this time, I still really miss this place. Jesus Christ, I miss it. I think about it everyday. I even dream about it, I miss it so much.

– Rick Chopp, Timmins, Ontario

Primal Fear

Steve Guindon never had a chance. He was cleaning drill holes out of the face when the walls of stope 5635 exploded in his face. One minute the world was as it should be – Steve Guindon and his partner Glen Harwood had just finished lunch over a laid-back chat about the upcoming Christmas break. Then they'd headed back to the drilling face. Guindon was at the face while his partner Harwood was running the jackleg drill. Without warning a rock burst hit the stope.

Guindon took the force of the hit, falling back onto his partner. Harwood didn't even know what hit him. One minute the world was as it should be, the next he was lying in complete darkness calling out for his partner. That's when he felt the faint fluttering on top of him. Then the fluttering stopped. Even in the darkness of a mile-deep tomb, Harwood was conscious enough to realize that Steve Guindon, friend and partner, had just died on top of him.

Harwood was totally buried in rock – his right arm bent completely behind his back, his left arm fully extended in front of him. He could hear the hissing of compressed air through the broken drill hose beneath him. That air was keeping him alive, extending his torment for how long? He felt himself fading. Letting go in the final moments. Thinking of his wife Shirley. Thank God the house had been paid. Thank God he had insurance. And then in his mind he saw his little girl Veronica. She was crying in front of the Christmas tree. Crying out for a father taken just four days before Christmas. And then his mind shook off the numbing balm and he began screaming for help. But trapped as he was in a mile-deep tomb, nobody could hear him.

To professionals who make their living working behind a desk, it's known as an event. The term covers a host of terrifying underground spectacles; the seismic shifting of millions of tonnes of ground; the sudden movement of a fault line tearing up underground tunnels and work stations like an elephant busting a tether; or the sudden release of ground pressure in the rockburst that blew apart the world of Glen Harwood and Steve Guindon.

The gold fields of Kirkland Lake are notorious for events. The gold is found in narrow fault zones running like underground streams. The surrounding rock formation – syenite porphyry – is hard, brittle and notoriously unpredictable. It has the tendency to shatter like glass.

The event in stope 5635 hit at 2:20 pm on December 20, 1991. Immediately the mine rescue squad began assembling. Heading the Macassa Mine rescue squad was veteran shift boss Eddie Obradovich. He was joined by fellow shifter [shift boss] Brian Pascoe.

Once they reached the 5600-foot level, Obradovich led the rescue team along the narrow manway ladders into the damaged stope. They were shouting out to Steve and Glen, hoping against hope that voices would respond. Harwood was trying to call out. He wanted to see his little girl and his wife. He wanted to be free of the blinding pain that was slowly squeezing the very life out of his hands and legs.

But the rescue team had to move very carefully. First they had to assess the damage in the stope and then slowly, painstakingly they began to remove the pieces of blasted rock. Finally they'd managed to breach a small tunnel in order to get fresh air down to Harwood. Minutes ticked into hours. Realizing that Harwood could give up before they freed him, Eddie Obradovich laid down on the muck pile and pushed through the rock until he found Harwood's hand. He held on, literally, for dear life.

"Hold on Glennie, we're coming for you."

Harwood's arm was pinned by the drill hose which was still connected to the drill buried below him in the muck.

"We can't get you out, Glen," Eddie told him. "It's gonna take time. We gotta free your arm."

"Cut it off," Harwood croaked. "Cut the damned thing off."

But mine rescue weren't leaving until Glen Howard came out in one piece. They needed to keep him conscious.

"Don't you fall asleep on me you son of a bitch. Stay awake. Stay awake."

Obradovich and crew were shouting, pleading, cajoling, threatening, until after six hours of careful digging, Glen was secured to a stretcher and hauled up through the manway. Harwood's days underground were over. His legs were permanently damaged, his back secured with a brace.

The death of Steve Guindon shook up the tightly-knit mining fraternity of Kirkland Lake. Guindon's sister, Sue, didn't want her own husband Rob to keep working underground at Macassa. But Rob Sheldon wasn't leaving Macassa, not after he'd already played his luck card by moving to Macassa Mine in the wake of his friend Steve Nixon's death at the Kerr Mine in neighboring V-Town (Virginiatown, Ontario).

Still, Rob tried to reassure Susan. The way he saw it, he had one of the safest jobs in the mine – working on the cable bolting crew. After a stope section had been mined out, the cable bolters moved in to secure the back with cable bolts and timbers to act as a bulwark for the tonnes of mixed rock and cement which would be poured in as backfill.

Sheldon's partner was Leonce Verrier. A veteran gold miner, Verrier's world centered on his family, especially his young granddaughter. Verrier had more than enough reasons to be proud of her. Having her tug on his arm to read her stories had given Verrier the courage to finally take the big step to swallow his pride and fight his life-long illiteracy. At 42, he'd learned to read just so he could share in the simple pleasure of sitting on the couch and reading children's stories.

But Verrier was worried. He confided to his daughter Lise Bernatchez that he thought the mine was getting more dangerous. He was working down in Stope 6723, a region that one shift boss described as being "in one of the worst areas of the mine. The stope was huge, probably too big and there were two weak faults on either side of the stope."

The size of the opening, a 200 x 45 foot cavern, was indicative of the new longhole mining techniques being used at Macassa. Longhole drilling blasted out 75-foot openings, compared with a mere 8- or 10-foot "cut and fill" slices taken out by the old handheld jackleg drills.

Macassa mine owners Lac Minerals needed the longhole drills. At 60,000 to 80,000 ounces of gold a year, Macassa was a steady and reliable producer. But such returns didn't mean jackshit in the gold world, where eating your way up the corporate food chain was the only game in the business. Competing against much larger, low-cost producers in South America and the Third World, Lac had to boost the production levels – hence the move to bigger and bigger stopes deep underground.

The mine relied on backfilled cement which was poured into the mined-out breaches. The cement offered, at most, about 3,000 pounds per square inch resistance when the surrounding rock pressure was at least 10 times as great. For a crew working in between these two "slips" of ground, it was like standing on wooden staging perched between to two colossal freighters. If one ship moved, everything in between would be torn loose in an instant.

It was just after eight in the morning on the morning of November 23, 1993. Kirkland Lake mothers were returning inside after watching the little ones get on the school buses. That's when the plates started to rattle in their cupboards. In Kirkland Lake, the rattling of the plates in the kitchen has always been a sign that men were dying below. And sure enough, 6,700 feet below the town, one of the rock faults near zone 6723 suddenly moved, tearing up the cable bolts, bending timbers and crumbling the cement paste ceiling. Thousands of tonnes of rock and broken cement crashed onto the world of four miners – Leonce Verrier, Rob Sheldon, Dave Kitty and Nelson Bourgeois.

"I got the call from the mine early in the morning," recalls Darlene Verrier, wife of Leonce. " They said Leonce and Rob were trapped and it may take an hour to find them. Then it was two hours. Then a day. And then it just went on and on and on."

By mid-morning the mine office had begun to fill up with frightened family members. All that was known at this point was that there had been three consecutive bursts, all down around 6700 level. Two men, Robert Sheldon and Leonce Verrier were still missing.

As mine rescue assembled, management were defrieting with Nelson Bourgeois and Dave Kitty to try and find out what happened. Both men had been there. Both men had managed to get out. Dave Kitty had a reputation of a sixth sense for danger. Kitty's tingling must have been in play that morning. He'd just started to climb the manway [a narrow vertical tunnel with a ladder] out of the stope to take a piss when the first rockburst hit. Kitty found himself scrambling up the manway as the ground literally collapsed behind him.

Bourgeois had been at the far end of the stope when the first burst went off. He'd immediately dived into a vertical metal culvert that was in place to pour down the cement backfill. Bourgeois jumped into the culvert to escape the rain of rock. He escaped out of the stope as the culvert was crushed below him.

Lise Bernatchez found out about the accident in the late afternoon. She was in Sudbury (350 km south) and her mother had been frantically calling all day but Lise had been in class at college. By the time mother and daughter spoke, Darlene was an emotional wreck; Dad's missing; you have to come home; we don't know anything more.

Daylight was quickly disappearing from the winter skyline and a snowstorm was brewing. When Lise finally reached home, the news had gone from bad to worse. The mine had initally said it would take the better part of a day to locate the men. But once mine rescue reached 6750 level, they saw the magnitude of the blast and were forced to reassess their plans.

The Sheldon and Verrier families – including sons, daughters, uncles, sisters, cousins – were bunking down for the night on the mine office floor. Every miner's wife knew the odds diminished drastically for every hour that was spent trying to locate trapped miners. It was a race against time. And as each rescue team returned to surface, the family members were there waiting, hoping against hope for news. But the news wasn't good. The supporting ground pillar [unmined rock used as structural support] had been shattered. All the main access routes into the stope were blocked with tonnes of broken rock. Even more ominous was the fact that the ground continued to let off smaller, nerve-shattering bursts as the mine rescue team gingerly picked their way through the rubble. The company announced that a much larger rescue operation was needed. Over 50 men volunteered.

Management was now looking at a four day-rescue. People told themselves that it was still possible. Maybe Rob and Leonce hadn't been injured. Maybe they had water. The four-day target, however, was soon pushed back to six days and the families were moved from the mine office to a nearby motel. But as the sixth day approached, Mine Rescue had to tell Darlene and Susan the bad news – everything had ground to a halt. After painstakingly removing 175 tonnes of rock from the ore pass, the rescue team was confronted by a complete blockage. A slusher machine [a metal scoop blade controlled by a motor and cable] had fallen into the pass during the initial burst and was totally lodged in amongst the broken rock. The blockage was 60 feet up the pass. One miner climbed the opening carrying a bag of AMEX blasting powder. He wired the powder as the ground continued to sputter and burst around him. He then carefully climbed back down. The blast went off but the slusher remained jammed.

Mine Rescue are trained for situations that rarely take more than a day to handle. Now they were moving in on a week of round-the-clock, nerve-shattering work. The tension was felt all over town. In the mornings, wives of mine rescue men headed into work with increasingly dark rings under their eyes. Restless children couldn't pay attention in class. Nobody slept soundly as long as husbands, dads and sons were crawling around in the depths of that shattered rock face.

A team of psychologists and grief counsellors were brought in, but they were wasting their breath. Northerners don't cry on the shoulders of outsiders. Don't expect mining families to sit down with strangers and share their feelings. It just doesn't happen. Eventually the support professionals gave up and went home.

On Day 11, over 2,000 people came from across the region to an outdoor prayer service. They stood in the shivering dark night and sang Amazing Grace. Candles were lit and placed in a field of snow. That night though, management delivered the bleak news to the families – the ore pass was being abandoned, the crews being pulled back. The supporting ground pillar was simply too shattered to allow men to continue working in this zone. There was no hope for a rescue. From here on in, the process was being renamed a "recovery operation."

"The motel bills of keeping the family and relatives near the mine had begun to mount," recalls Darlene Verriere. "And as the rescue continued to drag on and on, mine management said they wanted us to go back to our homes and leave the motel. I said, 'Fine. I've got a van. I'll sleep in the parking lot of the mine because I'm staying until you find him.'"

The story disappeared off the newspaper pages. Life began to return to normal. For the mine rescue teams and the Verrier and Sheldon families, however, the nightmare stretched into weeks and then into months. The January 6 target date had to be blown off and 10 days later mine rescue had to admit more obstacles. Tired of what she thought was the run around from management, Darlene showed up one night at the home of mine rescue leader Brian Pascoe.

"I want to know what's going on down there. I want some answers."

Brian didn't have anything he could tell her. Darlene wasn't one to be blown off. She showed up again the next night at Pascoe's place with some of her daughters. Sitting on the couch in Brian Pascoe's living room she demanded to know the truth of what was happening underground. He tried to tell her how it was like digging into a giant pile of sand. Every time they pulled out rocks from the bottom, more fell down from the top.

"For the longest time we had hope, that they (Leonce and Rob) had managed to hide or that they had water," recalls Lise Bernatchez. "The mine kept telling us they were getting close. We were so anxious. Why haven't they found them? What are they doing down there? But when we saw photographs of what the rescuers were up against, that's when I knew there was no more hope."

On January 21 the team was held up by another "substantial obstacle" – the remains of a scoop tram couldn't be moved because of the unstable ground. Rescue teams were now blocked only 14 feet from their target. The crews were forced to back up and begin drilling a second access route – the No. 1 drawpoint – which would bring the rescue team out in front of the blocked scoop loader.

At 5:30 am on of February 11, 1994, a body was found in stope 6723, just west of No. 1 drawpoint. Six hours later the second body was located under a large piece of broken quartz. It had taken 77 long and nightmarish days. The only comfort was learning that it was clear the men had died immediately. The burst hit them with its full force. They had been crushed completely.

Following the funerals, Rob's brothers, Steve and Fred Sheldon, continued working at the neighbouring Kerr Mine. On June 2, 1995, Fred was pinned by a piece of muck while running a mucking machine on the 2650 level. He died on the cold, muddy ground of the drift as medical teams drove to the mine. He was 42 years old. The Kerr Mine closed a year later.

In 1999, Macassa Mine was shut down following a series of rockbursts that blew apart the No. 3 Shaft below 5,700 feet. Common wisdom in the mining community accepted the view that the once-prolific gold fields of Kirkland Lake had breathed their last.

In 2002, the derelict Macassa Mine was purchased by a junior mining company at the fire sale price of $5 million. Following an agressive drill program the company discovered numerous new gold zones boasting some of the highest gold values ever found in this 90-year-old mining town. The mine is now valued at over $250 million and 300 miners have been hired to work in the restored operation. One of those who signed up to go back down was Darlene Verrier's new husband, Brian Pascoe.

"I thought a lot about going back," he says. "Darlene and I have talked a lot about whether it was a good idea..."

He pauses as she pats his hand supportively.

Pascoe is a gold miner. Going back down is just something you do.

Death of a Son

Nobody prepares you for losing a child. There's no book that's been written that can help you. Chad [Lamond] had wanted to be in mining since he could breathe. It was in his genes from birth [he was a fourth-generation hardrock miner]. He'd light up when the talk around the kitchen table would turn to mining. He'd block everything else out.

Chad was 20 years old when he died. He had already been mining for two and a half years. He was working with the contractors. They were driving a ventilation raise at Creighton Mine. It was very warm and humid at that level. They are supposed to supply ventilation to these areas – it's on the list of things to do, but it's just not very up there [as a priority].

Two nights before he died, I had a dream that he had fallen down the shaft and died. The accident happened on March 7, 2002. I was at work that day and at twenty after two I suddenly decided to leave. I don't know why but I left work and headed home.

I was coming around the corner and I saw the owner of the contract company standing there with some of the contractors. They were all just standing outside my door. I knew right there that something had happened.

I started screaming, "Is he dead? Is he dead?" I just didn't want them to tell me he was crippled or suffering.

What do you do then? I wanted to go to the scene. I wanted to identify the body. They kept giving me the runaround. Nobody would tell me the truth. They were saying they didn't know where the body was. The police finally called and said, "You don't want to identify him." Nobody ever told us anything. One minute they say he was here [drilling on a platform], the next minute he was gone. He fell 800 feet.

The undertaker told us that it had to be a closed casket. They didn't want me or anyone else to see him. I wasn't allowed to identify my son's body. But I was the first one to see him born. I wanted to be the last one to see him go.

I said, "I don't care what you have to do, you put him back together. It's going to be an open casket."

If people didn't want to go up to the coffin, that was not my problem. Too bad. The funeral home had to redo his face, put on ears, and his hair.

There was an awful lot to do in the lead up to the funeral. I cleaned. I made coffee for people coming over. They came over from morning until night to bring us food. And then suddenly it all stops. Then it goes in the opposite direction [with people saying], "I thought you wanted to be alone."

Chad's girlfriend Carrie [McKee] was six months pregnant at the time. She used to drive Chad to work every day and pick him up at the end of the shift. The day he

died, she had a doctor's appointment because they had been afraid she'd lose the baby. Chad wanted to stay off work and go with her. She said no, they needed the money. She could deal with the doctor on her own.

She was sitting in the parking lot of the mine waiting for Chad to come out. She was watching Mine Rescue and the police going in without knowing what had happened. Finally someone recognized her and brought her into the mine.

After Chad's death Carrie stayed with us for close to a year. Evan was born three months after Chad's death and it was like a miracle. He was so much like Chad. My husband lives for that child. Still, it's bittersweet. Carrie is young and she's now getting on with her life. You realize how careful you have to be because Chad isn't here any more to smooth things out.

It's hard to go to work but life goes on. Your co-workers complain about things but you don't care about the little things like you did before. You've been through a war and you just don't fit in any more with the life you once had. You only fit it in with people who have been where you've gone.

– Kathy Lamond, Dowling, Ontario

Twilight for a Shaft Sinker

Hughie MacInnis is lying in his bed, his nearly naked body partially covered by a comforter. He's lying on his side because the bed sores on his back have become an open and seemingly unhealable wound. Two years ago he had special surgery on them after the holes became so big you could literally fit an orange in them.

If only the sores would heal, then Hughie might be able to get out in his wheelchair. On good days, he can make it in his electric chair all the way down the road for services at the church. More and more, though, the days are spent here in the bed. But Hughie doesn't complain. Instead, he does what he has done so much for the past 28 years, he watches TV. Today he's watching a rerun of Kelly's Heroes and he knows all the parts.

When I come in, Hughie gets me to sit near him and we start trading Cape Breton place names. He was born in Judique, near Inverness, a great-grandchild of the tightly-knit Scottish clans who came to Cape Breton Island during the dark years of the Highland Clearances. I tell him about my mother's family – Clan MacNeil from Iona near the Bras d'Or lakes. My grandfather left Cape Breton for the gold mines of Timmins when he was 17. A generation later, Hughie followed the same road to the uranium mines of Elliot Lake.

"What brought me here? It was the job. It was 1957 and I heard they needed men in Elliot Lake. I was 15 years old."

The Elliot Lake mining boom exploded from a few exploration tents to a wide-open, out-of-control boomtown at the height of the Cold War. By 1957, 12 new mines were feeding the United States military's obsession with securing as much uranium as possible. Costs were no object. The U.S. government was paying cash on the barrelhead for anything the mines could produce. The only catch was the mines had to meet the strict production schedules or forfeit the contracts to other mining zones scrambling to bring uranium mines into production.

With a shortage of skilled miners, the companies were paying wages unheard of in the other mining regions. Anyone with two legs, a strong back and no fear could get a mining card. Word quickly spread along the impoverished rural roads of Cape Breton. Hughie and his Dad joined the exodus to Ontario.

Home in this new land was a bunkhouse of 26 Cape Bretoners.

"You had to be 18 to go underground but some of the Cape Bretoners who were already working lied for me. They said I had been working with them for years in Newfoundland."

The shift boss didn't believe a word of it. "If this is how he looks at 18," he said sarcastically after seeing the youthful Hughie, "I'd hate to see him when he turns 50."

Nonetheless, the shifter turned a blind eye and within a week, Hughie MacInnis was working on the shaft crew at Panel Mine.

It was a wild time. Pay cheques were regularly lost in bunkhouse card games. Brothels operated out of roving panel trucks which simply pulled up alongside the bunkhouses on payday. As many men were being killed speeding along the bush road into Elliot Lake as were being killed underground.

"The Nordic Hotel opened in September 1957," says Hughie. "Two guys were killed the very first night it opened. The first guy was killed after he got into a fight over the fact that someone took his chair when he got up to go to the washroom. The second guy was killed in an argument over the brand of beer he'd ordered."

Hughie's dad didn't make the cut in this tough world. The teenager drove his unemployable the 2,000-kilometre trip back to Cape Breton and then drove all the way back himself to continue his job. By 17, he was an underground crew leader.

The quick expansion of the Elliot Lake uranium mines created fertile ground for contract companies looking to bid on new development projects. Veteran contract kings like Paddy Harrison competed for jobs against the up-and-coming MacIsaac brothers from Cape Breton. The MacIsaacs, Hugh and J.C., were notorious for their inability to work together. They competed against each other harder than they ever fought against anyone else.

Hughie initially went to work for Hugh "Blue Eyes" MacIsaac who ran a company called Drevo Contracting. Blue Eyes and his partner Findlay Walker always hired Capers [Cape Bretoners]. And they expected them to produce. When the Elliot Lake boom collapsed in 1959, the contract crews moved their operations to the expanding nickel mines of the Sudbury basin.

"I started on a contract at North Mine in Sudbury. I worked 12 hours a day, seven days a week. I worked every single day for three months without a break," Hughie recalls.

By this time, Hughie had married Shirley MacDonald, a nurse from New Brunswick. They were starting a family and had settled into Sudbury.

In the early 1960s, Hughie broke from the pressure of the Drevo crew and went to work as a "union" man – punching the clock in the Falconbridge No. 5 Shaft. He lasted eight months. The pay of the contract crews was too good to turn down, and Hughie, still in his mid-twenties, liked the life of a highballer.

He then went to work for the other MacIsaac brother – J.C., owner of MacIsaac's Drilling and Tunnelling Company. When it came to shaft sinking jobs, J.C. maintained a Cape Breton crew, a Finnish-Canadian crew and a "Heinz '57" gang of French Canadian and other workers.

"J.C. was a great one to work for," says Hughie. "I had gone three years without a holiday, but I didn't have to fight for one with J.C. If you got your footage [tunnelling targets] you did okay."

Get your footage. Meet the targets. This was the secret of a successful contract crew. J.C. trusted his front-line men to get the job done fast, efficiently and without getting anyone killed. Contractors have a reputation for breaking all the safety rules. Hughie insisted on a clean and orderly worksite. Just as in the children's game of rock, paper, scissors, Hughie knew that in the world of steel, rock, flesh that flesh would lose out every time.

In 1975 Hughie took on a job deepening the No. 7 Shaft at Inco's massive Stobie Nickel Mine. It was the last shift of the year and Hughie was looking forward to packing the year in and taking Shirley out for an early New Year's Eve bash.

With half an hour left on the clock, the only thing left to do was to adjust the cryderman clam shovels which would be used to muck out the next blast. The shovel blades were operated by cables extending down from an operator's cab. Hughie was standing on top of the cab adjusting the cables when a younger member of the crew stepped into the cab, causing the machine to bolt forward. Hughie was thrown down the shaft. He fell 70 feet and landed, back first, on the iron-molded jaws of the clam. By the time the crew had scrambled down to the shaft bottom, Hughie was turning blue – suffocating on broken teeth that were trapped in his throat.

Hughie was immediately flown to McMaster Hospital in Hamilton. His T-10, T-11 and T-12 vertebrae were completely smashed. His back was a mess of bone fragments. He had two blood clots in his brain. He was also suffering from brain swelling – the result of bone fragments pushing against his cerebrium.

He lay in coma for two months, his lower body turning the colour of blueberries from the clotting. Shirley, with four children back in Sudbury and a job to maintain, took the all-night bus down every weekend to sit by his bed.

One day he suddenly gained consciousness.

"I was like a two-year-old child," he says. "I didn't even know my own 13-year-old daughter when she came up to the bed."

The family had to spoon-feed him. They had to teach him who he was and slowly explain to him what had happened. For the longest time he thought he was still a youngster suffering from a hockey accident.

Hughie came home after six months. Then began the fights with the compensation department to get proper lifts in the house for the crippled young man with four children.

Shirley was 37 years old and a veteran nurse. She knew their life would never be the same again.

"I told him when he came home from the hospital that he couldn't take it out on us. It wasn't our fault."

By and large Hughie adapted, but it wasn't easy. Shirley explains, "If he managed to come down in the morning in his wheelchair and then needed a bowel movement, I'd have to shoo the children downstairs. Then I'd have to lie him on the living room floor and clean him up."

Hughie was a big man who was now totally dependent on his wife. She nursed him through numerous bladder infections and other complications from the accident.

But for years she carried the bitterness of wanting someone to account for what happened to her man. She blamed MacIsaac's. She blamed the crew man who caused the accident.

"He never even came by to say he was sorry," she says, her dark eyes flashing.

But then she softens. "The man's mother was a very religious woman. She prayed and prayed for us. I know she did. Her prayers helped me learn to live with what had happened."

Life went on. Hughie's children grew. J.C. MacIsaac continued to cover the family's medical and dental benefits. He always invited the family to the annual Christmas parties held at his house.

When Hughie's son needed a job, J. C. hired him on but he never let the young MacInnis go down with the underground crews. "I couldn't face Shirley if anything happened," J.C. told him.

When MacIsaac passed on the business to his own son, however, the MacInnis family were written out of the company portfolio like a forgotten debt. They never heard from the company again.

"How do you do it, Hughie?" I ask. "How do you manage to hold on living day after day, year after year in a bed?"

The question surprises him. "I always think to myself – tomorrow's going to be better. You know, you got to remember there are people out there who are worse off than me."

Downstairs the grandchildren can be heard bounding through the house. It is Sunday afternoon, and like so many traditional Cape Breton families, this is a day for the family get-together for a feast and lots of laughs.

On the way out, Shirley stops me. "Thanks for coming," she says. "It does Hughie a lot of good to be able to talk about the old days."

On the wall by the main entrance there is a wooden plaque that reads:

*"Where there is faith,
there is love,
Where there is love
there is peace.
Where there is peace
there is God.
Where there is God
there is no need."*

First Woman Underground

As a battered wife with young children there weren't a lot of options of charting your own way as a free-minded woman in a mining town. You couldn't live on your own. People thought you were either a lesbian or a slut. They didn't see that I was willing to work in the mines because it would mean I didn't have to live on waitressing tips and could afford to finally take my kids skiing on the weekends like other people. People saw this move as a very threatening gesture.

There were people who jeered and said I couldn't make it. But there were men who weren't afraid to give me a chance and admit me to the mining fraternity. One of these men was my friend Sonny. He was such a man's man. He taught me to walk every inch of the way underground. He taught me that the big picture was just many small pictures. Without him I wouldn't have made it. But he believed in me and said you can make it. When the miners made me part of this inner circle they told me their secrets.

The miners knew the score. They knew that if they had x number of years working with uranium and the radon gas they were going to die. They knew these things. The men wouldn't tell the women when they began to get sick. But the women knew. The wives knew that if you work on the crew, you fish with the crew, shop with the crew and if one of the crew gets sick, the other members of the crew will be getting sick as well.

I remember one miner who had found out he was dying from lung cancer. He came up to me and said, "Carrie, just look after my old lady." The issue of cancer in the Elliot Lake mines wasn't just a union problem, it was a family problem and these men were my family.

I know that it's patronizing to say but I truly loved my miners. They were my guys; they believed in me and I believed in them. The only way I could repay them was my ability to read, write and fight for their families to get compensation. It was an unwritten law that I would help their families and that's what I did. The miners gave me that confidence and I carry this confidence to this day.

– Carrie Chenier, Elliot Lake, Ontario

Lovers in a Dangerous Time

Bill Whelan:

I was driving truck for $8 an hour and was away from home five days a week. When the chance came to get hired on at St. Andrews Gold Mine I went to the trucking company and told them I had the opportunity to go into mining. The mine offered work near home at $16 an hour. I wanted to know what I should do. They said, "What's there to consider? You're crazy to even think twice about it."

I went to work in 1997 at St. Andrews at the age of 30. I was a crusher operator in the mill. We were working the night shift with a skeleton crew in the crushing house. I had been working for the company for exactly two years when I went to work on the night of September 19, 1999. It was 10:35 at night and I was doing a circuit check when I noticed a wire hanging over from the moving conveyor belt and I reached out to try and remove it.

The wire caught my right hand and the belt pulled my arm through and ripped it off right to the shoulder. If there hadn't been guards in place on the side of the belt I would have been pulled in up to my head. If it had been my left arm that was pulled through my heart would have been pulled out along with the arm.

When it happened I remember thinking, "Do I fight or do I just lay down and die?"

I stuck my hand into the wound in my chest and grabbed whatever I could to try and stop the bleeding it felt all velvety. What I didn't realize was that I had grabbed my brachial artery. I was holding it between my finger and my thumb. If I hadn't done this I would have bled to death.

When I started to go and find help the first guy who saw me screamed and ran away. Sam McGuire was the lead hand on shift that night and he started the first aid.

Trish Whelan:

The accident happened at 10:30 but I wasn't told until midnight. I was the last one to know. His brother, his sister, his mother – they all knew. None of the guys from the mill wanted to call me. I guess they didn't know what to say. Bill's mother called me from the hospital. I was alone at home with two-year-old Liam. My mother took Liam and my father drove me the hospital. By this time they had gotten Bill stabilized and we flew down to Toronto Western Hospital at four a.m. I phoned his best friend Pierre the next day to tell him. He was driving truck and he pulled over on Highway 400 and just cried like a baby.

Bill Whelan:

I was in the hospital for 11 days. The surgeons tried to reattach my arm but there was just too much damage to my chest and back. When I woke up after surgery I realized what had happened. I began to think – what do I tell my wife? What do I tell my family? What have I put my family through?

I was afraid about coming out of the hospital because I was afraid of facing Liam. What is he going to think of me? I'm no longer a whole person. But I remember when I came home from the hospital, he came in and said, "Hi Dad," and then he went out to play.

I then went to use the washroom. I was sitting there and I couldn't wipe my ass. I called out to Trish, "What am I going to do?"

She said, "Deal with it."

Trish Whelan:

We had to get on with life. He had to learn how to bathe himself. He had to learn how to get dressed. There was no sense worrying about it. I wasn't going to do up his jacket for him. He had to learn how to do these things himself.

Bill Whelan:

For the first while I relived that moment every day. I beat myself up over it. How to change what happened? This went on for a year. And then one day I heard Liam ask Trish a question and it all hit me like a ton of bricks. I was sitting on the couch in a catatonic state and he asked, "Is Daddy going to be like this forever?"

I realized I needed help. I needed counselling. I went back to college. I'm getting retrained. I really think there are a lot of opportunities for me.

Trish Whelan:

I told him, "So you lost an arm, big deal. You move on. You're alive." Some people couldn't understand how I didn't mourn the loss of his arm. I didn't marry his arm. It wasn't part of his personality. It's just like if he puts on weight. Does this change the man I love?

Into the Deeps

It's a 31-kilometre round trip from surface to the 7400 ramp level at the Kidd D Mine. We're doing the drive in an air-conditioned suburban with leather seats. Stompin' Tom Connors is playing on the CD player. Hugh MacIsaac (a new generation of the famous shaft sinking MacIsaac clan) is in the driver's seat. I'm riding shotgun. Somewhere down below the 3,000-foot ramp level we pick up a hitchhiker – a contract driller. In no time at all, the two men break into spirited discussion about, get this, the techniques necessary to master the art of barefoot water skiing. Here we are, driving through the diesel mist, discussing the thrill of cresting the surfaces of glacier lakes in bare feet.

On any given shift there are 20 pickups hauling crews to various work areas. In addition there are numerous haulage trucks and road graders making their way along this underground roadway. Above the 6800 level, there are nearly 600 workers hauling over two million tonnes of copper/zinc ore a year from the main Kidd ore body. From 6800 down to the 8000 level there are another 400 contract miners building the infrastructure for the new Kidd D Mine project. The centerpiece of this expansion is an $85 million shaft job that will bring the mine to a depth of 10,200 feet, making Kidd D the deepest base metal mine in the world. In addition, there are 35 kilometres of new drift development being undertaken at a staggering cost of $4,000 a metre.

By the time it is done, the Kidd Mine will have more underground thoroughfares than the nearby City of Timmins. The cost of building this underground city is tagged at $640 million.

Hugh MacIsaac has seen a lot of mine projects but even he is awestruck by the size of a project that he describes as "mind boggling."

"A project like this comes along once every 25 years," he says. "It's hard to even describe the magnitude of the expansion."

The development of Kidd D speaks to the changing nature of Canadian mining. The original Kidd Creek ore body was a fabled discovery. In 1963, a single exploration drill hit a massive sulphide ore body rich in zinc, cadmium and copper ore. Initially the ore body was thought to be in the order of 25 million tonnes. Given the richness of the deposit and the ability of the original owner - Texas Gulf Mines - to retrieve the ore with hydraulic shovels and pit trucks, it was a licence to print money.

By the late 1960s two fundamental changes were made that transformed the nature of the Kidd operation. First, the mine began the move to underground mining as geologists realized that the ore body was many times larger than originally thought. Secondly, political pressure from the surrounding region resulted in the company agreeing to build a world-class smelting and refining operation. The Kidd Metallurgical Site provided infrastructure that encouraged further exploration and the commitment from Kidd's subsequent owners (Falconbridge and now Xstrata) to provide copper and zinc feed from operations as far afield as Chile. The smelter operation has provided the surrounding region with hundreds of stable, well-paying jobs.

By the late 1990s the future of both the smelter and the mine were in question. Nearly 125 million tonnes of ore had been taken from the deposit and the existing mine was thought to be in its sunset years. Tantalizingly, however, deep drilling confirmed that the ore body continued into the depths. The question was, what were the possibilities of mining zinc-copper ore at levels two miles deep?

Ground pressure and heat have always been the two significant barriers to mining deep. And yet, the geological "architecture" of the ore body naturally mitigated against these problems. Unlike many ore deposits, which run as stringers and veins through the fault lines of competing ground structures, the Kidd ore body is shaped like an immense plug. Because of the plug-like nature, the surrounding ground doesn't exert the same seismic stress encountered when mining out veins. The stable nature of the ground has allowed the mine to carry out deep mining employing massive blast hole mining stopes in the nature of 60,000 tonnes.

The second factor is that, despite the intense heat underground, the temperature is actually cooler than other mines found at similar depths. Mine Manager Dan Gignac explains: "There is a 17-degree-Celsius difference between our ground at 7400 level and the ground at Creighton at the same depth. The Kidd ore body is much older. It's had a chance to cool. Unlike the mines in Sudbury, the Kidd ore body wasn't created by a meteorite smashing into the earth and releasing all that hot magma."

The lower ground heat provides a major boost in the company's bottom line because 70% of the mine's electricity costs are tied up in providing cool air ventilation. As Ontario's single biggest purchaser of electricity, the Kidd Mine and smelter operation is very much susceptible to any rise in electrical costs at the operation. Quite simply, the cooler ground at Kidd Mine may just keep the aging giant alive.

The mine managers will tell you that, just as the nature of mining has changed, so has the kind of miners needed to go down in the cage. "We're a giant rock factory," one of the managers explains, "We need to find ways of encouraging youth to see mining as an exciting job requiring brains not brawn. We don't want the old style miners any more. We want college degrees and young people into computers."

Maybe so, but the miners who are taking the mine into the depths remain very much cut from the mold of the fiercely independent bonus miners of old. After one shift, I'm sitting in a bar drinking a beer with a second generation Finnish-Canadian shaft sinker and I put the question to him – why would someone work on a shaft project two miles below the Earth's surface?

His response is straight to the point. "Every day I tell myself I should quit but every day I go back. Why? Because it's what you do. It's like I know that this job is making history."

The Grand Farewell

It's barely noon and we're already on the third course of a five-course meal. There's king crabs lightly touched with butter and lemon; scallops bigger than any I have ever seen; live lobsters bumping against the edge of a plastic bucket; two pots of water boiling on the stove – one for the crustaceans, another for the pasta.

Complementing the seafood is a plate of fresh bread and the offer of wine – a cool, semi-sweet, white German with a dainty drop of dew on the side of the bottle. No thanks, I politely say - raising my glass of water. Water is hardly an appropriate aperitif for such a feast but the perspiration on the wine bottle is certainly more attractive than the sweat dampening my brow and sticking my shirt to my chest. I'm tired, hung over and the weather is suffocatingly hot. Not like a Labour Day weekend in the north at all.

Last night, after the sixth bottle of Molson's, the idea of celebrating the "Last Supper" seemed like a brilliant idea. Mario Gagnon had announced it was his last weekend in Canada. He was buying the drinks. He was the one who came up with the idea of inviting us all over to his house for a Sunday afternoon fish feast. And we, the cluster flies hovering around the energy of that bar room table, had agreed.

But then these promises had been made on a Saturday night when minute-old friendships promise lifetime bonds. It's now Sunday and none of last night's partiers are anywhere to be seen.

As I pick at the food, I try and reconstruct the faces of my "best friends" from the night before. There was the waitress – "She passed out here at about five," says Mario in his thick French-Canadian accent, "Right 'der in the hall." There was whatzisface from Kidd Mine and his girlfriend, as well as the writer from the paper. They all came back to the house after the bar closed, but Mario can't remember them leaving. No matter, he assures me, as he tries to ring the barmaid on the cellphone, they'll be back.

After all, we're celebrating the final weekend of a long, hot summer. We're celebrating his farewell to Canada. The party will happen. The people will come. And once the feast is over, Gagnon, a 44-year-old underground mine mechanic from Quebec's Gaspé region, will place his Harley-Davidson motorcycle into storage, load up his tools and head to Mexico.

Everything around us, from the large black couch with the matching love seat to the wine glasses and the large TV/home entertainment unit, will be left behind. This comforting illusion of domesticity has been rented, one month at a time, with the anticipation that when his contract is over, there'd be no strings attached. That's the secret score of mining. Get in while money is flying and get out before the sad goodbyes. Gagnon's life is a literal embodiment of this cautionary tale.

He learned his trade as a copper miner at the age of 17 in Murdochville, Quebec. As soon as he could, he jumped to a job at a mine in Leaf Rapids, Manitoba, leaving behind a community that would eventually be left as an economic basket case when the mine at Murdochville was closed. Gagnon never looked back. He signed on as a mechanic leader on a shaft sinking crew and was soon traveling the world. He's done tours of duty in Tunisia, Brazil, Venezuela, Argentina, Bolivia, New Mexico and Alaska, as well as virtually every mining camp in Canada.

Mario's latest job was as a leader on the Kidd D shaft sinking project. But Mario won't be around for the completion of Kidd D. He's now leaving for a two-year stint, hired by a South African mining contract company to oversee a crew of Chilean shaft sinkers at a gold mine in Mexico owned by Canadians. In Mexico, the work will be 12-hour days, seven days a week with no breaks for two or three months at a time - pretty much the same life he's had here in Timmins. Only there, the weather will be warm and the beer cheap.

But on this last weekend in the country, Mario doesn't want to talk about mining; he wants to talk about lobster. It brings him back to his childhood in the fishing culture of the Gaspé coast. I can only nod at the details he provides me on what makes a good lobster feast. After all, what do I know? I'm just a "fish sticks on Friday" Catholic with a throbbing head.

The man is perfectly at home in a kitchen that, despite a weekend of partying, is kept immaculate. The kitchen utensils are gleaming; the surfaces scrubbed; everything in its place. Is there a woman in the picture?

Mario laughs. Yes, somewhere in this story there was a wife, but she's long gone. "It's not much of a life when you're gone for four months and see her for one month," he says.

Mario handles his own domestic duties and keeps impressive order. It is, I suppose, the way it has to be for a man overseeing the maintenance of drills and machines on a shaft job. Shaft sinking is a matter of life and death and Mario, the master mechanic, has to ensure that nothing is overlooked. The days when a miner was killed on every new shaft job are over. His job is to ensure that nothing goes wrong with the production schedule.

"There's no downtime allowed," he says. "Every day you gotta make a bench [a blasting level]. After every shift the jumbos [hydraulic drills], the clams [large scoop shovels)], everything has to be checked and maintained. You sign off for everything you do."

The stakes are simply too high for anything to go wrong. Mario has seen it all. He's helped haul the broken bodies out of an underground rockburst at a shaft job in Brazil. He had one good friend taken out by an errant blast in the Hemlo gold fields of Northwestern Ontario. "He goes in one day and kaboom, now he's in a wheelchair for the rest of his life."

The danger of a shaft job seems so far from the white tiled kitchen where Mario is pouring hot pasta into a colander. Yet tomorrow morning he will turn in the key and shed this domestic skin just like he has shed so many past lives before.

But what will he do when the two years is up? Will he simply pack his bags and head off to somewhere else – Africa? Asia? The Arctic?

"I might retire after this one," he admits. "I'm getting older. I don't want to end up on crutches."

He muses vaguely about what he'd do without mining. Perhaps move back to the Gaspé. Perhaps open a tourist hotel.

But then, Mario puts the line of questioning to an end. "You know," he says. "I've got no regrets. Shaft sinking was my education. It allowed me to see the world. It's been good to me."

By now a few stragglers have begun to make their appearances. The phone rings. It's the waitress and her friend. They'll be over later. Looking forward to the big send-off.

The sun on Labour Day no longer stays as high in the evening sky as it did just a month before, but the breeze is warm and there will still be time for tales of the deeps and lots of drinks as we catch the final dying rays of the last summer weekend in Canada. In a mining town, everybody knows that when the highballers are moving on, it's always time for a good party and a grand goodbye.

[As this book was being finalized Mario Gagnon contacted us to let us know he was back in Canada and working on the Nickel Rim shaft sinking project in Sudbury, Ontario.]

Mining Town Reprise

Even when they were shutting the last mine down in Elliot Lake, many miners believed there would be another one found. I think this optimism is fundamental to people who deal with the raw elements of the earth. You see it in the fishermen who can't believe the resource has been depleted. Miners are of the same ilk. But when the mines did close, there was so much hardship, so much pain. People lost their pride and their marriages. You saw people pulling out in the middle of the night with their trailer and they were gone forever. Our community was dispersed.

We all came to this town with nothing. We said we were going to stay two years and make a fortune. And after 20 years we left with nothing. All we had left was the memory of the good times - the dances, the curling bonspiels, the way we looked out for each other's children. It's a sense of community that I don't think we'll see again.

The miners and their families did so much good work in that town. When you think of the miles that were walked for local charities, the money that was raised for the hospital. The town now has a big Mining Museum and it tells the story of the owners. Who is going to tell the story of the miners?

It was a good town. Physically it was killing us, but emotionally it was such a good, good town. We were privileged to be there.

– Carrie Chenier, Elliot Lake, Ontario

Driving a ramp with a jumbo drill, for the Kidd D Mine expansion, 8000 foot level, Kidd Creek Mine, Timmins, Ontario.

Field Work for this book took place between 1991 and 2003.

The following is a list of those who were interviewed or who provided assistance:
J.J. Biloki, Joe Bardoel, Claudia and Angel Breton, Lester Beattie, Lise Bernatchez, Felix Brezinski, Hans Brasch, Carrie Chenier, Carlo Chitaroni, Rick Chopp, Alfredo and Angela Ciccone, Connie Comtois, Eric and Landa Cormier, Armand Coté, Reg Doan, Moe Durocher, Mike Farrell, John Fera, Mario Gagnon, Rollie Gauther, Dan Gignac, Wayne Glibbery, Rick Grylls, Vern "Tooey" and Irene Haluschak, Dwight Harper, Dick Hunter, Dan Hutchinson, Bernie Jaworsky (author of "Lamps Forever Lit"), Andy King, Wilson "Newfie" Lambert, Kathy and Rob Lamond, Bill Lee, David Lee, Mick Lowe, Claude "Shaggy" Ludgate, Hughie and Shirley MacInnis, Marie MacInnis, Hugh MacIsaac, Cory McPhee, Mary Martyn, Susan Meurer, John Miller, Jack Murnaghan, Alex Perron, Brian Pascoe, Shirley Picard, Danté and Carla Piccoti, W.T. (Red) Phillips, Frank Ploeger, Tom Ranelli, Jack Rauhala, Scotty Robertson, Pete and Glenda Saille, Anne and Ralph Schmidt, Homer Seguin, Steve Sheldon, Moe Sheppard, Jerry Stewart, Don Taylor, Hughie Vallance, Ed Vance, Darlene Verrier, Bill and Trish Whelan, Steve Yee. A special thanks to all the miners, mill and smelter workers we met along the way on surface and underground. We apologize for anyone we may have left out.

The Following Companies and Unions Helped Provide Access:
Aur Resources, Northfield Minerals, Falconbridge, INCO, Deak Resources, Placer Dome, Rio Algom, United Steelworkers of America Local 4440, USWA Local 6500, USWA Local 7580, Mine Mill / CAW Local 598.

The following mines, mills and smelters were toured:
Astoria Mine, Cheminis Mine, Clarabelle Mill, Copper Cliff North Mine, Craig Mine, Creighton Mine, Copper Cliff Smelter Complex, Dome Mine and Mill, Falconbridge Smelter, Garson Mine, Kidd Creek Mine, Louvicourt Mine and Mill, Macassa Mine and Mill, Pamour Mine, Stanleigh Mine and Mill, Strathcona Mine and Mill, Stobie Mine. As well, the Kerr Mine and Mill was toured extensively over several years.

The following strikes were visited and studied as part of this project:
Dome Mine strike 1990, Giant Mine strike 1993, Falconbridge strike 2000, Horne Smelter strike 2003, INCO strike 2003.

The photo editing is based on the invaluable advice of John G. Morris and Ken Light with additional perspective provided by Erin Elder, Moe Doiron, Don Weber, Patti Gower, Brian Kerrigan and Stephen Bulger. Special thanks to Jean Francois Leroy, Alison Nordstrom, Jon Levy, MaryAnn Camilleri, The Globe and Mail and PDN for giving the project the initial support and exposure. We also would like to acknowledge master printer Andre Laredo and Anthony Reinhart for editing the text. Thanks to Kirsten Rian, Chris Rauschenberg, Photolucida and Critical Mass without whom this book would not have been published

For more information visit: www.louiepalu.com and www.charlieangus.ca

Louie Palu and Charlie Angus gratefully acknowledge the funding provided by the Ontario Arts Council and Canada Council for the Arts for portions of the fieldwork for this project.

ONTARIO ARTS COUNCIL
CONSEIL DES ARTS DE L'ONTARIO

Canada Council
for the Arts

Conseil des Arts
du Canada

Back cover: Steve Allen sitting in front of a CAVO 320 mucking machine,
1450 foot level, Kerr Mine, Virginiatown, Ontario.

As part of photolucida's Critical Mass, Hiroshi Watanabe, Sage Sohier and
Louis Palu were each awarded monographs by a group of 200 jurors
comprised of some of the most important photography curators in the world.
To find out more about photolucida, Critical Mass, the other two
monographs and our Portland portfolio reviews go to:
www.photolucida.org
ISBN 978-1-934334-02-7